THE PORTAGE POETRY SERIES

Series Titles

Lost and Found Departments
Heather Dubrow

Marginal Notes
Alfonso Brezmes

The Almost-Children
Cassondra Windwalker

Meditations of a Beast
Kristine Ong Muslim

lost
and
found
departments

Poems by
Heather Dubrow

Cornerstone Press
Stevens Point, Wisconsin

Cornerstone Press, Stevens Point, Wisconsin 54481
Copyright © 2020 Heather Dubrow
www.uwsp.edu/cornerstone

Printed in the United States of America.

Library of Congress Control Number: 2020936165
ISBN: 978-1-7333086-2-5

This is a work of fiction. Names, characters, businesses, places, events, and incidents are either the products of the author's imagination or used in a fictitious manner. Any resemblance to actual persons, living or dead, or actual events is purely coincidental.

Cornerstone Press titles are produced in courses and internships offered by the Department of English at the University of Wisconsin–Stevens Point.

DIRECTOR & PUBLISHER   EXECUTIVE EDITOR   DEVELOPMENT COORDINATOR
Dr. Ross K. Tangedal   Jeff Snowbarger   Alexis Neeley

SENIOR PRESS ASSISTANTS
Monica Swinick, Jeremy Wolfe, Heidi Propson, Brendan Gallert

SPRING 2020 STAFF

McKenna Rentmeester, Olivia Frome, Johanna Honoré, Aleesha Splinter, Ali Zamzow, Tori Schuler, Colin Aspinall, Dartaja Carr, Lindsey Bundgaard, Kelly Barrow, Kyle Beattie, Dylan Morey, Sarah Sartell, Tara Sparbel, Lindsey Strike, Brianna Stumpner

For Don,
whose love enabled us to find so much that had been lost

Also by Heather Dubrow (as poet)

Forms and Hollows

Border Crossings

Transformation and Repetition

Poems

SIGN LANGUAGES
Taking It With You   3
Boarding Calls   5
Speaking in Tongues   7
Here Comes the Bride   9
Notes from the Underground   10
A Narrative about Lyric   12
Sea Changes. After Ovid   13
Left Out To Dry   15
Corporate Rodents   16
Hidden Agendas   17
Inventory of Arsenals   19
Important Jewelry   21

AUTOCORRECT
Autocorrect Repair Shop   25
Dietary Restrictions   26
Reversals   28
Con Games   29
A Calendar of Yesterdays   30
Curricula Vitae (I)   31
Curricula Vitae (II)   32
In vino versitas   33
Risks of Inserting an -IV-   34
Orange Harvest Moon   35
Would you like our Sancerre or our Côtes du Rhone, Sir?   37
Hide and Seek   38
Bedside Manners   39
Guards and Guardians   40

ABSENCES AND HAUNTINGS

Riddling   45
Department Meeting   46
Family Histories   47
Mourning, Four Months Afterwards   48
In Memoriam   49
Class Reunion   53
Independent Contractors (I)   54
Nuclear Test Site (I)   55
Bedtime Stories, or, Fragments from the 1950s   56
Spring 1968   58
Guess Who's Coming to Dinner   60
Ghost Story   61

FOUND IN THE FIRST FOLIO

Falstaff Recast   65
Puck (I). Puck to the Changeling Boy   66
Puck (II). Puck to his Agent   68
Strawberry Fields Forever   69
Lear's Fool   70

FORMS LOST AND FOUND

Art Nouveau 1905   75
Art History 101   76
Sweet Dreams   77
To Catch a Thief   78
Aubade for our Early Evening   79
Nuclear Test Site (II), or, Damaged DNA   80
The Syntax of Insects   81
Cemetery of Lost Plots   82
The city pigeon   83

ACKNOWLEDGMENTS   85

SIGN LANGUAGES

"When I use a word," Humpty Dumpty said, in a rather scornful tone, "it means just what I choose it to mean—neither more nor less." So he failed first grade but won the Yale Younger Poets prize.

Taking It With You

"Please use trash receptacles or take it with you"
Sign in Beacon, NY train station

i

Back there where
     Eve's basil plant was more fragrant and more full
     than her apple tree
     but never too full of itself, never sneaky enough
     to snake into another herb's bed

          ("climate change is responsible for the
          disappearance of the entire species")
Back there where
     the two slept dreamlessly seamlessly—most nights anyway till—
     still in the only bed they could dream of
          ("for graves have learned that woman-head
          to be to more than one a bed" John Donne, *1572-1631)*

Back there when
     the waterfalls ran smooth as lullaby
     never gushing and they hadn't heard of rushing
          ("yes, the pledges in our rush gotta run fast
          with backpacks for all five miles—but my
          God how could any of the brothers have
          known that his heart—")

Did she even notice
     the pinpricks of insects nested on the basil's stem
          ("all we found were little pinpricks of the cancer")
     where they slept but never harmed the plant,
     so she never needed to say goodbye
     to it or anything else.
     Not yet trashed herself,
     she never knew from trash receptacles—
     "please use trash receptacles"?
Come on, folks, this is Eden.

ii

You can't take it with you?
They hadn't really needed to take the basil plant—
God was generous enough with herbs in the fallen world.

The other insects also came along for the ride,
perched on leaves from an apple tree,
girding their own sticky loins
for their tasty new gardens.
And the funeral directors found that trashy Lilith's photo
               stashed in the receptacle of Adam's pocket.

Boarding Calls

"All passengers must control their bags at all times"
Sign in airport

i

Look, here's my boarding pass—
right here—
and a passport documenting everywhere I have been.
I am *all passengers* from back there to tomorrow.
But will they let me board while I am hoarding memories
in a bag much too big for the carry-on rules?

ii

Must control? Give me a break.
I wrote the book on it (Ithaca, NY: Cornell University Press, 1970).
I'm into controlling
        the most mischievous of erroneous endnotes,
        the settings of my upscale coffee machine,
        the ending of my ghazals.
I am monarch of witty puns,
my fourteen-year-old no longer green-streaks her hair,
and I control fantasy till it turns couplet.
But memory has legs
and this bag has legs—
dashing out of line in the airport,
diving from the overhead compartment
right onto my crown.

Control must's? I need to fly from
the mapping   the misses   the mastery
of tomorrow by what happened yesterday.
I— not they— will master *must*,
fasten its seatbelt,
and arrange a smooth landing.

iii

But *at all times?*
Makeup does wonders for the bags under my eyes,
        though not for the dreams that caused them.
Thanks to therapy and poetry
I no longer pack heat for the roasts and broils
        at family dinners

5

and even keep bag and mouth shut
during Thanksgiving toasts.
I can control my baggage
in conversations with my children
                    (most conversations anyway).
And I can turn dagger into joke
                    ("what a wag she is").
But *at all times?* No.
Not during the midflight turbulence,
                    not during the midnight sleep roaming,
and not when we land back home in back there.

Speaking in Tongues

"Welcome. Please choose your language"
Sign in CVS drugstore

i

Welcome to the last month of the marriage.
Please choose your divorce lawyer and
rephrase your accusations.

Choose? This language chooses its victims:
I mutter, he mutters, we mutter
$\qquad\qquad$ about each other.
Muttering is in a different dictionary
$\qquad\qquad$ from nattering,
a weighted book in my backpack.
These sounds choose us $\quad$ use us
in their world without passports.
Mutters are the unsaid the undead doing their calisthenics
$\qquad$ inside our rosy mouths
until we can no longer shout or explain or sing.
No lawyer dare oppose
the exclusive territory they claim.
Our court date is set.
Happy Mutter's Day.

ii

Welcome to your hell. Please choose your linguistic
symptoms.

My neighbor was as crisp as the pastries she baked
when she first moved next door,
feisty as the jokes she told me then.
Born in Germany, emigrated young—
she lost all speech after her stroke
except the one she spoke
when she was just a girl
and seldom since.
Reclaimed, chosen by her native tongue
or frozen in it to keep her other paralyzed limbs
company as they try to trudge
to their first home.

iii

Welcome to your family holiday. Please choose
your cutlery and your cutting words.

Do the teasers know or care
when tickling words inflame bare skin?
Or rejoice
at their choice?
Please choose your language,
knowing well that malarkey
rhymes conveniently with snarky.

iv

Welcome to the museum exhibit.
"According to Native American beliefs,
spirits communicate with people
through whistling."

Please choose to join these spirits:
whistle with them while they work.
That's not wind but the language
they are asking me to hear—
knowing it uncaps antidotes
to the secreted bile in teases,
knowing that it sings to
she who has lost her bearings
as she tries to bear
words' games of hide-and-seek.
Come, hailed by their whistles,
hear throughout your legal hearings
melodies clearer than those hassles.
Yes come, hear all their whistles,
for these wordless songs will guide me
beyond this wilderness of words—
beyond attacks disguised as archness,
beyond words ironed down with legal starches—
to where words are spirited again.
Hear and hail these whistlers
and choose freed words once more.

Here Comes the Bride

"Warning: scaffolding is alarmed"
Sign on building under construction

Look: the bridal gown is dyed to eggshell white
the wedding scrapbook lies through its teeth
about all those yesterdays and about tomorrow
one cake's poisoned flower is another man's meat
Tide detergent makes bruises bright
something new, something blue? no need to borrow.

Listen: some stains even German washing machines give up on
                and trousseaus are nonstarters as scaffolding.
Skyhigh twin towers of tomorrow's bliss
coupled like the figures on the cake and
scaffolded with promise
the clouds' master jeweler engraved in sand

        I do
I will
           I never will
                  again
I'll always try

See the good fairies dancing in those magic rings
bestowed in a sky-blue bag from Tiffany.

With scaffolds like those, who listens to the wind
        sirening through the towers
or to the rain
        crying down those posted signs
and who will heed
girders scaffolded with signed—

HARD HAT AREA

REPORT UNSAFE CONDITIONS TO

—warnings
for those who could not read the alarming signs.

Notes from the Underground

[first screen] "Train schedule is not"
[second screen, after a few seconds] "available"
Sign in 86th street 4, 5, 6 subway station

i

God wrote the book in stone,
        and on the eighth day made the trains run on time.

OK, team, SO LET US NOW PRAISE FIRMEST SCHEDULES:
Schedule
      your mammograms,
      your Candy-grams,
      your birthday cards,
      your privet hedges,
      your policies from Travel Guard,
      your tax return fudges,

          your assignments, your cosmetic refinements,
          your tax-deductible consignments,

            your restaurant and ethical reservations,
            scholarly endnotes RE the League of Nations.

Study
        how to make schedules in a Number 1 pencil,
        how to soothe the past onto padded scented hangers
        in a walk-in not trip-in closet
        where it will exit only by invitation,
        how to braid into answers the whistling in your ears,
        how to file memories like recipes
            to be extracted after careful consideration
            on family holidays and other special occasions
            and served warmed, but never aflame.

Let's hear it
        for applications for jobs and apps for maps
        for dreams that always keep an eye on wristwatches
        for questions that always hold their knees together
            when they wear short skirts.

Teach
>your household help to arrive at 8 AM prompt
>(the laundry room is empty then)
>and your college students to meet deadlines
>(not halfway either).

GIVE ME A "D"   **"D"**
GIVE ME AN "E"   **"E"**
DEADLINE, DEADLINE RAH RAH RAH

Bombers and bombshells, sexy and otherwise, are denied visas
to this country of schedules,
>whose borders are guarded
>with watches and watch towers.

ii

>But remember:

schedules
>*skid*

even God can't schedule orgasms.

Caesuras interrupt the corporate board meeting
when they think it's the catering service knocking.

Pace Julia Child's instructions and maledictions,
>soufflés still surprise and are surprised.

So for God's sake, abandon schedules if
a slice of moon or of a smile
>or an art opening
>is
available

>in the galleries of gleaming *may be.*

A Narrative about Lyric

"your lyric machine"
Signature on message automatically generated
by scholarly organization on lyric

i

Lyric machine?
But lyrics and cats have little patience for machines.
OK, so the right stroke— yes, right there— will usually generate a purr.
But lyrics and cats can turn purr into growl
at the flick of a tail
or when tailing a flicker of truth.

ii

Lyric machinations? Fair enough.
In tenth grade you thought lyrics had model posture—
          the dentist every six months
          pay your estimated taxes on schedule
          and just in time every couplet tells it like it is.
And then you learn lyrics posture, gyrate,
masticate madeleines
into angry crumbs Proust wouldn't recognize.

iii

~~Your~~ *My lyric machine?*
It owns and disowns its poets.
And how many machines have you met
that wink at you
to let you know that with its permission,
on rare occasions,
you can close your eyes and see?
My lyric machine?
Yes. "This thing of darkness I
gratefully
acknowledge mine."

12

Sea Changes
After Ovid

"owner: Orpheus Management Corp"
Sign on building under construction

Right after Eurydice's snake berefted him, broken ("till death do us part" indeed), his old college roommate texted him: "Terrible news about your tragedy— let's go out for a drink." Said roommate suggests he be fixed up with that roommate's wife's sister and with a nice job in the guy's real estate firm, which is flourishing despite its cutting some corners. Orpheus said no to the sister but yes to the job offer. And the skills that had entranced those creatures in the forest worked so well for him as a landlord that he soon persuaded the wolves in the banks to float him enough money to launch his very own management company.

But the more deals he works in the underworld of management, the more he thinks about Eurydice in her underworld. So before too long he makes a deal (at a loss) to sell his new management company to the roommate and accepts the deal the gods of the underworld offer him to reclaim his beloved.

Poets are into refrains, but this, tragically, is a different kettle of fish. Play it again, Sam? He cannot refrain from looking backwards, and so the plot swirls back to the loss of Eurydice once more. Does he try to comfort himself with same-sex relationships or decide to have a hot thing going with his lute, or just mourn again, silent and silenced? Depends on which version you read.

But in any event, we know that before too long those drunken Maenads launch his fatal voyage, dismembered. His music seems to sink, silenced forever. Schools of fish stare appalled at his rapidly bloating body and his head floats, bleeding, into the next plot line

where entranced MFA candidates remember his story and the year he almost beat Dylan for the Pulitzer Prize in poetry. So they fish out and claim his head as their relic in the hope, vain of course, that it will help them get jobs and pay off the loans for that MFA lest they become lyrical deadbeats. Yet

13

his lute has a life of its own and, remembering his dismembered
fingers, it plays without him

still plays— still—

his favorite songs, which float into and out of my memory as I try to
edit this.

Left Out To Dry

"Feel the power"
Xlerator hand dryer

Power makes and breaks promises, kneecaps, lunch dates. Power
Often scrolls on its phone while we speak truth to power.
As he saws his team in half, this corporate magician glowers.
Count the empty desks and do the math to see his power.

The chef's voice raises chills without being raised too much:
His sweating, chopped up staff can hear his power.
Who knew his joke could have such punch
In its victim's mouth? Taste blood. Taste wrath. Taste power.

Trophy wife wheedles him to buy spicy
Platinumed perfumes. Smell her path. Smell his?/her? power.
The black gowned arm descends. Kid sacrificed.
Power feels him up post-bath. Feel power.

Can poetry disarm all those harming hands?
Dubrow hands you this. With ruth. Hoping poems too have power.

Corporate Rodents

"Shop till your mouse drops"
Amazon advertisement

A mousetrap from Amazon warriors? Well, drop
Your dough into its maws. Shop till your credit rating drops.

Mother cat: "No mouse until your bowl's licked clean.
OK now— here's dessert—don't drop."

His agent nixed 'Of Mouse and Man':
"Keep thinking, John, think more." Then the penny dropped.

Hire a mouse to test mousetrap cheeses.
Shop till his union complains or your mouse drops.

The mouse goes broke from those late-payment fees.
But the poet keeps squeezing the words, drop by drop:

As in—his August head cold makes him moan,
"Our damned climade is almost dropical."

Or Julia Child to her would-be clones:
"Your soufflés rise each time, but your mousses drop."

Poem, what if you disappear in my shady Dell?
"No worries, Heather. Trace me by my mouse droppings."

Hidden Agendas

"seriously sharp"
Label on a type of Cabot cheese

Teasing a child,
like tickling a child,
plays hide and seek
with *fun* and *funny*
while *cruel* hides in plain sight—
sharpening its cleverness,
famed for its deviousness.
It wins all its playground games:
singing ever louder,
swinging ever higher,
much too close to the child's head.
Who plays by the ground rules
when swinging so high
in playgrounds like those?
And memory's smartphone records all the smarts.
       Smile and say "cheese" even during the teasing.

Teasing a child
sports a clown's makeup
pretending   lending   bending   pleasure
while concealing
who gets the pleasure,
and while revealing
who has the power,
whose words curdle
while arms cuddle,
who knows all about breaking and
who doesn't put on brakes.
       Can't you take a tease?

No. Let's serve instead
at well baked family dinners
the creamiest risottos
when would-be resentment
can melt in the mouth.

But if rebuke is necessary,
serve a private first course
of the *seriously sharp*—
always accompanied by the milk of
kindred's kindness.
                    Milk that never curdles.

Inventory of Arsenals

*"For three generations,
Aggressive Shade, Glass and Mirror
Company has guaranteed workmanship
and customer satisfaction."*
Website of a successful company

Aggressive Shade?
Nonsense—shade is relaxing
with a glass of rosé in its hand.
It knows melanomas are a no-no.
It cornered the market in sunsets,
and looks the other way
when aggressive glass and mirrors
as usual don't leave a tip.
Hey wait a minute—
haven't you heard about "throwing shade"?
You haven't been to my department meetings
or met the chair so full of himself
that he tried to climb out of this stanza
and take over the whole—

No, it's my poem, dammit, and now I'm writing about
Aggressive Glass.
It dismisses Tiffany whites as moldy,
taught LaFarge everything he knew
about those self-satisfied blues of his.

OK, let's try on *Aggressive Glasses* for size instead.
My designer is bigger than your designer.
I can afford these frames
because my firm was aggressive on Wall Street.

Well, how about *Aggressive Granny Glasses?*
Granny here made brass knuckles out of pasta,
and cooked the toddlers soft-boiled eggs for dinner
but put on her big round spectacles to help her
read hard-boiled detective novels to her sweethearts for dessert:
"Alice, Jerry, come look and" —

19

Granny is turning the page and pushing up her glasses—
"see the dismembered corpse."
"And what do you think the detective said
when he kicked the perp in the balls, honey?"
They don't make grannies or glasses the way they used to.

Aggressive Mirror?
"Mirror, mirror on the wall. Who's the fairest of them all?"
"Enough with the rhymes," the mirror cracks back.
"My college roommate is a plastic surgeon, and I've talked him into a discount for you.'

Important Jewelry

"important jewelry"
Listed in announcement about auction

announces its presence,
pronounces its importance,
renounces price tags as vulgar
(and of course hardly needed
by those who matter,
those in the know).

The blue of Tiffany shopping bags
was co-opted from the sky
by a lawyer specializing
in Mergers and Acquisitions.
Heaven forbid those bags
should talk with their mouths full,
or raise their voices in public places.

They were raised
by the right sort of families,
knowing their level voices will silence
those not on their level,
and, my dear, advertising is clearly
not the family business.

But this jewelry still broadcasts
its invaluable message
about these valuables:
those who proudly possess me
are the possessions
of those who bestowed me.
And my proud possessors
are possessed by
importance.

AUTOCORRECT

Big Mac Attack

The morning was a lot sunnier than my disposition. Business had been so slow lately I was beginning to think a bake sale might be the best shot towards paying the rent. In slinks a blonde whose rent a lot of guys must have been competing to pay.

"You're Mr. Michael Connelly?" she begins tremulously. "Can I trust you?"

"My ex-wife used to ask me that all the time. And you'll notice I said 'ex,'" I replied. "The people who have hired me haven't complained much, though we detectives, unlike restaurants, don't have sites where customers can post their reviews. So you'll have to decide for yourself."

And then her story comes spilling out— "Someone keeps stealing some of my letters when I type on my Mac and putting in ones of their own. My girlfriend said she thought some of the new words were Russian, but I know that Putin is a fine man, so I thought I'd better check with you."

I wasn't sure what in the back of my mind was bothering me, but something didn't sound right. She reminded me of the client who came into my office last month asking me to tail voices in her head that kept telling her to make intriguing typos and leave a lot of blank spaces. Her husband claimed the cat was jumping on the machine to make the typos, but she said she never let the creature on her desk.

"Let's start with your name, ma'am," I asked this new client. But rather than answering, she gets up abruptly, dropping onto my
                              desk a fw let   ters from her purr

24

Autocorrect Repair Shop

Autocorrect: cc'ing / icing

My Mac went to school at the Big Mac
and turned *goodfood* into *goofed.*

But Ovid had nothing on its next trick—
metamorphosing *cc'ing* into *icing.*

Icing wouldn't know from subtleties,
or for that matter from the decisiveness
of a neatly hemmed couplet.
It's not into niceties either:
it talks too loud in crowded rooms
and marches uninvited in Technicolor parades.
It never met a cake it didn't like.
As for its decorations:
            buttered and jammed in tastelessly and tirelessly.

On the other hand,
the motives of *cc'ing* can be crystalline—
or hard to decipher. Or challenging to find.

Cc sometimes wears matching shoes and handbag,
never leaving home without an umbrella,
never lies down without protection.

    Cc'ing checks the scores   knows the score
    predicts the weather   thinks through the *whether*
    covers the bases   uncovers its tracks
    so no one can claim to be blindsided.

Yet sometimes— for the *cc'd* reader
see see insists: look deeper, look quicker.
Is this *cc* a wink? or just a flicker?
        glinting hinting meanings bended
        towards what the *cc'd* party had suspected,
        often intending towards a shadow.

Dietary Restrictions

Autocorrect: meataphor / metaphor

Knowing all too well that revenge
orders its meat searing,
I visited many sites
that extolled the benefits of fishing
in scenic laid-back lakes
for the more predictable metaphors
gliding just below the surface.
And my cardiologist counseled
the lower cholesterol levels
in the sort of obedient poems
I wouldn't have dared to submit
to my Iowa workshop
(no accident that state is a major beef producer).

OK, let's hear it for
locally farmed metaphors,
swimming together in their containers
like the right sort of memories,
and yes, let's hear it for
angers so sedulously baked away
that a toothpick inserted in the middle
comes out clean and dry every time.
Remember that one man's steak
is a wiser man's editorial revisions.

That motorcade of flashing memories
exceeding the speed limit
morphs into this delivery boy
on his reliable bicycle,
bringing me language that arrives
warm but neither raw nor burned,
and always discreetly decked with dill.
Heaven forbid it should be meaty.

But wait—

at their hearts even these words
are rawer than seared meat.
And as for the health benefits of fish—
look again, poet, right here, at the end of these dangling lines—
creatures that bite and bait
their fisherman.

Reversals

Autocorrect: verses / versus

verses gliding towards my fingertips
that hoped to hold them and be held,
verses with their beckoning refrains—

are stopped blocked mocked,
locked up,
locked down,
by the electrified wall
built by the *versus* cop.

Con Games

From a letter of recommendation:
"a congenial and responsible colleague"
Autocorrect: congenial / congeal

i

Congeal likes nothing better
than to do a number on *congenial:*
     turning proffered iced tea
     into numbing shards of ice,
     kidnapping threads of conversation
     to knot them,
     and plotting against the microwave
     to coagulate the butter
     this machine had every intention of softening.

ii

Congenial, of course, would include *congeal*
     in its family Thanksgiving dinner
     (together with other second cousins once removed
     whom the less congenial insist on not sitting near).
     And *congenial* praises even
     the congealed cranberry relish
     when heaping it beside
     the rest of the spread.

iii

Watch out when *congeal* registers
for Creative Writing 101:
it can turn waltzing poem
     into hematoma.

But look—our couplet can have it both ways:
sometimes congealing
exploration into epigram.
But sometimes congenially
and respectfully
holding open for its readers
doors they assumed it would slam.

A Calendar of Yesterdays

Autocorrect: go / ago

DO NOT PASS AGO

> Pass? People like me always fail this test
> and don't stand a chance in hell
> when playing Monopoly with memory.
> We leave our umbrellas and our hearts
> in the corners of ago.
> As for the street repairs in ago,
> don't be fooled, as I was.
> They lie through the grinning teeth
> of their backhoe machines,
> which claim to remove the backup
> of yesterday's dirt and tar
> so that tomorrow's asphalt
> can smooth over the
> cracking cackling bad news underneath,
> and so the site supervisors
> can train the street lights here
> to run on time again.
> Smooth streets and smooth sailing?
> Finishing by tomorrow?
> No, it is the tomorrows that are finished,
> the uncovered trenches whose risks
> taunt us and haunt us
> despite the smooth-talking promises of asphalt.
> We still bathe our protesting sandals
> in dirt as loud as
> the words sung by memory
> during its victory lap:

DO NOT EVEN TRY TO COLLECT YOUR LIFE
    BACK FROM THE SAFE DEPOSIT BOX OF BEFORE

DO NOT PASS GO

Curricula Vitae (I)

Autocorrect: swell / as well

Or starts a shouting match next door,
while *as well* dines
on well-ironed linen
and well-manicured ironies.
And when *but* won't stop phoning,
the executive secretary of *as well*
regrets that it is in conference.

But the battle between *swell* and *as well*
is a whole different war story.
Swell a victim of Autocorrect? Give me a break.
Swell swats away that initial *a-* itself
and jerks together *s* and *well*
while grabbing the cab that little old lady hailed first.
As well is likely to wear ties
discreetly initialed with "a" and "w,"
but *swell's* shirt is open enough
to show off its hairy chest.
Swell delights in giving itself airs,
and could care less about the restrained initial "a."
Speaking of dropping letters, *swell* also doesn't worry
about getting into the college of its choice:
instead it flies first class
while forging letters of recommendation
fly-blown with words like *fabulous.*

The ancestors of *as well*
farmed the family plots in New Hampshire for generations,
always rotating the crops in time.
The closest *swell* gets to New England
is commandeering heaped platters of expensive seafood
in joints whose waitresses wear too much lipstick
and skirts cropped too short.

Curricula Vitae (II)

Swell slathers butter on its rolls,
serves overflowing casseroles,
leapfrogs rules,
won't suffer fools.
All those catalogues clogging mail?
It boasts of bargains it grabbed on sale.

As well typically orders one entree,
accompanied by arugula,
and by multigrain bread.
It disdains the lures of Restaurant Week.

32

In vino versitas

Autocorrect: verre (Fr. "glass") / verse

Spellcheck shatters glass of wine—
Burgundy's gold moon
slides into this liquid verse.

Risks of Inserting an -IV-

Typo: definite / definitive

definite put down its foot
definitive lays down
    the law
and holds up
    the traffic.

definite shops for digital books online,
definitive wrote The Book
                on stone tablets.

definite is into epigrams,
definitive considers rhymes and self-satisfied iambs
rather vulgar.

Insistence can be a smoke screen:
definite turns sullen and reddened,
choking on its own fumes.
And its icy assertions
risk frostbite.

When you put your money on *definitive*—
who always knows best—
remember that it lives in glass houses.
Yes, but it persuades even the mangy, ranging doubts
that were thinking of throwing stones
to come inside and polish those splendid glass walls.
Then pays them way below minimum wage
before deporting them.

Orange Harvest Moon

From "How New Humanities PhDs Fare,"
Inside Higher Education, June 11, 2018

*Humanities Ph.D. recipients in 2015 had relatively high job satisfaction
over all. . . . But there was an 11-percentage-point satisfaction gap between
humanities Ph.D.s working in academic positions and those working outside
academe . . . 56 percent of employed humanities Ph.D.s were teaching at the
college or university level as their principal occupations in 2015.*

Autocorrect: career / carrot

i

A field exuberantly growing
careers that will be harvested?
Or does that promised carrot
just glimmer on some hopefilled pond?

Veggie or algae?

ii

Look— so many universities
dangle that carrot
to feed their hunger for applicants,
to plump their thinning budgets,
to fool those who dream of lives in academe.
And yes, to fuel their hard driving faculty:
"My list of dissertators is bigger than your list."

Thus the egos
of faculty infectious with
puffy ambition
swell and redden,
bloated and boasting.
And thus they proudly brand
would-be careers with few buyers
in our heartless markets.

But don't forget the farmers
who take their work to heart:
plowing through dissertation chapters,
planting true seeds but not false hopes
with grad students they learn from and with.

And how about the programs that attempt
to diversify by rotating crops—
Professor? But maybe arts administrator, technical writer, editor. . .
Are these new carrots wholesome food?
Can this new menu sustain and be sustained?

Would you like our Sancerre or our Côtes du Rhône, Sir?

Autocorrect: relevant / elegant

Elegant could care less about
the determinations of briefcases
and the numerals on tax returns
that remember their mothers' injunctions
to keep their back and shoulders straight.
What it cares about instead
are sterling wordplay and salad servers,
and pedigrees with all their waltzing reflections.

Relevant never misses a train
and knows stainless steel will cut the mustard.
Relevant looks both ways at crossings,
but often misses a joke
(especially a pun, of course).

Hide and Seek

Typo: resist /revisit

i. *Revisiting*
He revisits his long-nursed hopes
when visiting the nursery.
He coddles his wrinkled ambitions
while cuddling his toddler.
Soon—birthday presents shiny in reflective paper,
with bows as determined as handcuffs:
bonding   binding   branding.

ii. *Resisting*
In weeding out family expectations
to free the self improbably budding,
to make room,
to make a room of his own,
to make room for his own,
rather than staying tied to the roots
in his family's tenderly tended garden—
the adolescent turns resistant:
dangles his legs over the rails
on bridges to nowhere,
grows marijuana weed and implacable rejections,
goes off the rails during Finals Week,
sports political placards,
won't play Dad's favorite sports.
And grows.

iii. *Returning*
Yes, but—new stanza   new room   no room.
Freud got it wrong
in so many ways
but knew damned well
that dead wrongs and dead parents live
and revisit us in new unintended plots.

38

Bedside Manners

Autocorrect: little /title

Which titles
entitle you
to belittle the listener?
He prescribes our first meeting from the get-go
with "*I'm Dr. Grandstand, Heather.*"
Will my "*I'm Professor Dubrow, Dr. Grandstand*"
cure or just insult?

Guards and Guardians

Autocorrect: doorman / domain

My *domus* is my domain,
where the location of
all light switches
and yesterdays
is always familiar,
where my keys and my Ghirardelli chocolate bars
are right here, right at hand.
In the home where I feel at home
I have dominion over everything
(except the cats, of course).

What doors are open
to the openers of doors?
The lobby is their domain?
They guard from would-be intruders
the doors of my world—
standing in their assigned places
in the lobby of the American dream,
repairing elevators
in which they had hoped to ride up.

"Sweetie, you should always say 'good morning,' not 'hello,' to Carlos"—
Small shareholders-in-training become familiar
with shared rules of etiquette:
when to avoid verbal familiarities,
to whom one hands out holiday tips,
and whose hand one doesn't shake.

> *And God said, Let us make man in our image,*
> *after our likeness:*
> *and let them have dominion over the fish of the sea,*
> *and over the fowl of the air*

and over
the doormen of their building.

The super's rules for his staff
include wearing white gloves.
Their white hands
and the white orchids in the lobby
increase the property values in our domain.

ABSENCES AND HAUNTINGS

Welcome back to Jean-Louis Memoire's award-winning restaurant, ma'am. For your amuse bouche today, we have the year before yesterday. Our featured appetizer is cracked eggs, prepared by walking on eggshells for too long. And would you like to hear about tonight's special entrée? Your celebrity chef cooks up regret beaten with egg whites until it rises sky high.

Riddling

"Knock, knock."
"Who's there?"
"There."
"Who's there?"
"Your here."

Department Meeting

Too many empty chairs and ears but
the room is jammed right to its ceiling
with living anger from earlier ruckuses
and from fights about dead causes.

       a jam that stains
       fruitlessly,
       marring recently laundered shirts,
       ensuring we wear old defeats on our sleeves.
       Clothes that uncover
       words long past but often rehearsed and never erased.
       A jam that crams yesterday into its cracking jars
       from which snarky cracks sneak out.

The meeting is called to disorder.
Some pale abstentions
are floated but sunk.
Ghosts of meetings past
are unanimously elected
to fill the position of chair.

Family Histories

*. . . died peacefully in her sleep Saturday, age 77 after a long illness,
surrounded by her family. She is survived by*

for her   the call   for them
                      long awaited
                      so many bells ringing

Will funeral baked meats
feed rest or nausea
to the loved ones who had feasted
on soufflés of clichés?

Will the airing of old ashes
and hollow scenarios of tears
ignite or dampen fires?

Unearthing all that dirt
disgorges
resentments once swallowed
but never buried.

Mourning, Four Months Afterwards

My spices still smell like old paper,
I furnish even my bedroom with briefcases,
if-only's blossom in the corners
of all my cellars.

But clichés show up on the doorstep,
suitcases packed for a good long visit—
He had a wonderful life
You have many happy memories
He was so proud of you—
They ring the doorbell,

                                  as self-confident as popcorn.

In Memoriam
For all the victims of autism, especially Adam R.

(Write it!) like disaster
—Bishop

i

An autistic teenager who cannot speak has been missing for a week
with no sign of the boy

AP, 10/11/13

"Avanti"= "Forward! Enter! Come in!" Use to invite someone into a room (Italian 115)[1]
     will this be on the final?
        was this his final

                        final
                            call to Avonte

       did his school fail his final
       by not recalling
       by not locking the door
       by not checking before

has he come into hallelujahs or horrors
has he come into his birthright
             born so wrong
                wronged so long

            has he come into the Kingdom of the Lord
        welcomed by the One who owes him
        the peace that passeth understanding

     or welcomed by the one
who beckons, who whispers to the speechless:
     Come in come here
           Avonte,
               Avanti
    do you reckon he came

---

1   *Introduction to Italian*, Lesson 7, p. 666.

inside their lair, to their luring
to their circle of hell
did they come inside him
is he enduring
does he still endure?
speak the unspeakable
for the one who cannot speak

fear capital offenses
while tabloids capitalize in boldface
on Avonte's thin face
and fortune tellers hiss their hunches

the Lost and Found Department
is out to lunch.

ii

Police in New York have arrested the 52-year old cousin of the unidentified dead child found 22 years ago and dubbed "Baby Hope"

The commissioner said the department had never forgotten the case and had never given up hope that the little girl's killer would be found.

"Detectives from the 34th precinct squad paid for Baby Hope's tombstone which reads at the bottom 'Because We Care,'" he said.

ABC News fall 2013

Baby Hope's hardboiled detectives
hoped hard and trusted

a tombstone that speaks   a suspect who spoke

Avonte's posters still shout the name of the speechless

fearing the unspeakable
who will speak hope now for Avonte

always silent   is he silenced

do they cover the mouth of the speechless when he
when they
Who is praying for Avonte
Who is preying on Avonte

Detectives paid to bury her body
Now the murderer is paying for Baby Hope

For Baby Hope trust was rewarded
for Avonte can we still hope and trust?

please answer:
let's foster and baby
our temples of hope

babyish hope?

iii

*Jan 21, 2014 - The New York City medical examiner said DNA tests confirmed
that remains found last week were of Avonte Oquendo, 14
www.nytimes.com/.../remains-found-in-queens-are*

always not here
Avonte returns in parts

Can we speak the part of departed Avonte?

iv

*Thursday, Feb 27, 2014 • Updated at 10:20 PM EDT
The medical examiner's office has concluded that the cause and manner of Avonte
Oquendo's death cannot be determined.
http://www.nbcnewyork.com/news/local/Avonte-Oquendo-Cause-of-Death-
Medical-Examiner-New-York-City-247341091.html*

trusty scalpels   truest of weapons
diligent doctors   dissect drowned tissue
determined technicians   drown him in solvents
                 the discovery phase?
Will lawyers discover

recover
the drowned one the found one
or drown him in words all over again?
Select an answer and mark the right circle.
His courtroom will be
　　　a) a factory for fabrication
　　　b) a wrestling ring for rights and wrongs
　　　c) a dissolving
　　　d) a resolving
　　　e) all of the above
　　　f) none of the above

Right it?
For Avonte.

Class Reunion

i

We are returning on June 8 by subway and cab.
They outwit doormen by returning unannounced
　　　　　　in the unhinged doors of midnight
　　　　　　in the syllables of light rain
　　　　　　on the fingertips of memory.

ii

Under the leadership of the Reunion Planning Committee—

he leadeth me

Our reunion luncheon will feature
comfort food.
　　　　　may we be comforted among the mourners of Zion

Please fill in the appropriate boxes and
return this slip to make your reservation
no later than May 27.
　　　　　they filled different boxes

Some committee members will show up early at the reunion luncheon in order to—
　　and some class members left early.

iii

You will be here
as our honored guests.
You will be there.
Charon took all your spare change,
but no worries about contributing to our class fund:
you've paid your dues.

Independent Contractors (I)

All readers in Fordham's
Poets Out Loud series must be reimbursed on
forms for "independent contractors"

i

independent?
Poems are as feral as memory.
Please don't feed the closural couplet—
it may bite and hiss
      when you wrap your hand or mind around it,
      anticipating a purring rhyme.

contractor?
But genre is a contract
no sooner signed than broken.
And the poets who apparently contract
vagrancy into tight-lipped epigram
      wink at the gremlins
      that slink between the lines.

ii
As for contracting memories of you—
      sorting, vetting,
      boxing,
      stitching, knotting
      until that first contract
      is forgotten,
      hemming away loose threads
      so no strings are attached any more—

Contracting the intractable?
Even I know better than to try.

Nuclear Test Site (I)

grinning trapdoors open
in tranquil groves of apples

who sprinkled fertilizer
on these cancer cells?

what snakes, what Eves, what Adams?

who baked the souffléd mushroom,
gift from that hottest oven
for Earth on Mother's Day?

and Who bled again when Earth was fed
                              in Nevada?

Bedtime Stories, or, Fragments from the 1950s

I scream
you scream
we all scream
for ice cream
he brings me chocolate-chocolate chip in the wrong bowl after her scream
    wakes me
and calls me their little queen
    and says Mommy just had a bad dream
when I cry and ask what's
                he gives me more ice cream

the next night he brings us ice cream again and he sings, *I'm the Good Humor man*
    with the ice cream kids all favor
    but that's silly
    he's the same Daddy, not the Good Humor man

I like Ike
They wear identical smiles for their children every morning and
they wear matching campaign buttons:
clearly a match made in heaven
Don't tell Daddy that your Mommy
    it's a special surprise that
        can you keep a secret, Sweetie?
        now that you're a big girl, I bet you can

I'm a good girl, I never told on her—
such a good girl she is, no trouble at all, even now—
but like her running mascara, gold stars stain your face

    It's Howdy Doody time.
    It's Howdy Doody time.
    It's time to start the show. So kids
and dads, *let's GO! On today's show, Princess Summerfallwinterspring*

    MY NAME IS ALICE
    AND MY BROTHER'S NAME IS AL
    WE COME FROM ALABAMA
    AND WE SELL APPLES.

No, it's her turn with the jump rope. You have to learn to take turns.
MY NAME IS BARBARA
AND MY BROTHER'S NAME IS BOB.
WE COME FROM BOSTON
AND WE
No, your father and I will take turns having you for Christmas.
MY NAME IS NELLIE
AND MY FATHER'S NAME WAS NED
WE COME FROM NEW YORK
But my mother said that even in New York I shouldn't tell
my friends that we were getting a divorce.
AND WE SELL LIES
On this jump rope it's easy to trip.

    Saying goodnight for Camels, America's favorite cigarette
he is smoking a lot
she never empties the ashtrays any more

bedtime stories are still read at her
till the final page
of theirs

I bet you don't even know. Cornelia's last name changed over the summer.
Her brother's too. You're crazy. How can a last name ever change? Except
when you get married. And boys' names never ever change. Her mother and
father got divorced and then— Divorced? Cross your heart and hope to die?
I thought that didn't happen much except in the slums and things

But my mother told me not to tell the other children at school because

Daddy loads a
               heartful of presents for them on
his visiting days
but the prize in the Crackerjack box bleeds.

Spring 1968

folk songs
and guitars
     as confident as Marimekko megaflowers

and chanting *hell no   we won't go*
strike   strike   we're all on strike
LBJ, LBJ   how many children did you kill today?

our hearts in all the right places,
our voices joined together at all the right rallies—
no longer joining the clangorous
crowds in the usual beer joints—
while our skill at draft counseling shielded
those born in the right families,
and while we chanted jingles
about those faraway jungles.

Choose a), b), or c):

a) My cousin the frat boy sent to Vietnam,
whose ROTC stipend had paid
for the beer at his parties,
was almost killed there, then reborn
as my cousin, the model citizen,
Emergency Medical Technician, male nurse.

b) My cousin the frat boy sent to Vietnam,
whose ROTC stipend had paid
for the beer at his parties,
was almost killed there, then reborn
as my cousin the walking wounded,
with his heart in all the right places now,
but his mind in a wheelchair,
wheels spinning,
turning   lurching   returning,

shoved backwards at corners
to what he left back there.

c) both of the above

Others paid much more:

>*where have all the flowers gone?*
>*to the biers of the boys*
>*who knew nothing of draft counselors and deferments.*

> *three helicopter strikes and you're out*

>*our Father who art in heaven*
>>*receive thy servant*

>*hollowed be their family*

strike   *strike*   *they are all stricken*
>*their father who was in Vietnam*
>>*did not come home*

Guess Who's Coming to Dinner

Would it work for me
to stay with you the nights of
Wednesday, November 8 and
Thursday, November 9?

First love as house guest?
Fifty years later, even one's husband
doesn't lose sleep over
who slept where back then.
I will offer corn muffins at breakfast
to the man I offered my life.

The doorman announces him,
memory, curdled into judgment, renounces him,

but now my husband opens the door,
pronounces the name that opens yesterday,
the name my colored dreams rewrite.

While he unpacks his suitcase,
I pack back there back up,
spreading, then refrigerating, the old blame,
      saber tamed into the hostess' butter knife.

Ghost Story

Forgers of handcuffs and of passports that never expire, what energetic world travelers our ghosts are. You can't leave home without them because you are their home, their only sunshine. They make skies grey just when you thought you were happy. All our armed guards and guardians—those aphorisms, those therapists, those chirping budding fibbing *fresh woods and pastures new*—are nonstarters at their security checkpoints when these terrorists decide to take our planes. Hey, Noah was too busy checking his caulking to notice that even the animals were tailed and trailed by specters.

FOUND IN THE FIRST FOLIO

A twenty-first century poet, a Shakespeare character, and her agent walk into a bar. The poet orders wryness on the rocks. The agent tries to tell the bartender that the character will have her usual, but she insists that neither he nor Shakespeare speaks for her— she is written by the culture, the material text, the audience, and is too often silenced when she attempts to speak. Announcing that a bar is no place for a scholarly lecture- not that there ever is a good place for one- the poet interrupts it by intentionally spilling her drink on the character. As the alcohol begins to create a sea-change into something new and strange, the agent announces that he still represents her, their contract just has to be renegotiated, and he will insist that anyone who casts her provide limousine service to the twenty-first century.

Falstaff Recast

My agent thought I had a good—
another round for these guys on me,
and sweetheart, you didn't fill my glass to the top last time—
shot at Lear, but that went to the buddy of the director.

Did you know my old man?
Expected me to join the family law firm
or become an army officer, Southern gentleman that he was.
(Heaven forbid his son should be an actor.)
His suits made to order
by those visiting tailors from Hong Kong.
Wanted me to marry some nice Wellesley girl
whose father would— His orders didn't suit me.
And hey, Dad, you think Mom and I didn't know
how much you drank sunk in those leather chairs
at the best club in the city.

> *Daddy-o, you Virginian patrician*
> *pisspot, you pitiful hypocritical*
> *litigator, you cologne drone you.*

The high school guidance counselor knew all about him,
warned me the children of alcoholics
become The Substitute Parent or The Fool.
Fooled you, Mrs. Mullarkey. Turned into both.
But thanks for introducing me to the drama teacher.

> *I'll play my father. "Harold, would*
> *you please bring another Chivas*
> *Regal, the Anniversary Special bottle*
> *the club has, for Mr. Westmoreland*
> *and myself."*

Puck (I)
Puck to the Changeling Boy

Son, first I interned as Oberon's Fool
(and got course credit from school for
      my raunchiest jokes).
But give me a break—
        McDonald's is a better gig than that.
Remember Titania's cute little fairies,
      who fed you dewdrops
         when you wanted Hershey bars?
Well, none of them would give me the time of day
            once they recognized me.
          (motley's the lonely wear).
And as for the big O.,
I kept my cards close to my chest
and dealt him conundrums and puns
        when he wanted me to deal coke for him.
Lord, what fools these immortals be.
Sure, I jested and made him smile occasionally,
but a Fool's jokes ripple and rumple and buckle,
      and an Oberon is into squashing and swashbuckling.
My tricks?
        The only ones he cared about were turned by those nymphs
(and when you get a little older, kid,
        I'll tell you all about him and Hippolyta).
So if you outgrow henchman,
and he tries to interview you for Fool down the pike,
      just say "maybe,"
and hold out for tuition to the college of your choice.

But last month I traded in my mercurial coxcomb
        for this Hermes briefcase
and became his personal assistant—
    Now I can fool the wisest aunt
        into investing in one of his derivatives.
And I fly first class with him when he hijacks the plot.
Our deals with the so-called regulators
      (those guys wouldn't know from a Fool's puns)

have even better legs than the stewardesses.
But listen, kid, when Daddy-O. isn't looking,
I still plant on the stony tablets of his spreadsheets
                                    bulbous green graffiti.

Puck (II)
Puck To His Agent

I wanted to be Caliban instead,
made it to the callbacks,
but couldn't stop punning.

Strawberry Fields Forever

Browsing Shakespeare's strawberries: is it easier to recognize his "spotted and inconstant man" or to discern decay on a spot check of a deceptive package of strawberries? "The strawberry grows underneath the nettle," intones the bishop of Ely, but what mold grows underneath the strawberry (or for that matter on certain priests underneath the bishop's supervision)? OK then, down to the corner fruit stand for some market research.

Another slippery slide: ripe, riper, rip-off. Even if you have a soft spot for good fruit, soft spots on fruit are a no-no. So I prowl all the fruit stands within three blocks now, wandering, wondering, gambling, grumbling. We all know that glowing clouds of white look great on Tiffany angels, but on strawberries it says time to move on. Is this red perky or febrile? Are the ones concealed near the bottom of the box soiled as a baby's bottom? My mother told me to wash my hands every time after I went and before every meal, but if you wash your strawberries too much before a meal, they start to go too. Like certain sonnets they slouch when turned, and they specialize in concealing base contagious clouds of mold.

Win a few, lose a few. Shakespeare's editors try to gloss those slippery strawberries. But let's hear it for the editorial staff of the kitchen, which turns the fruit stall's rip-off into a trim-off. A strawberry and a prune (all varicose veins and round shoulders) usually don't even talk to each other, but strawberries on occasions like this need to be pruned, revised, resubmitted to the bowl, then served with a glorious French crème fraîche sauce.

Lear's Fool

When knowing Lear but loving Lear
Makes a fool like Kent,
When daughter three will show no fear—
Sis buys but C. is spent—
When knowing all but loving few
Makes a Fool like me,
When seeing but not seeing through
Makes royal fools, while bastard E.
Sees enough to grab enough—

Then life in Albion will be rough.

FORMS LOST AND FOUND

"*I left a paradoxical encomium in my MFA workshop. Has anyone turned it in?*"

"*Before we start looking, do you have identification? We check more carefully now. There was a sonnet in the corner of the box for a long time, and suddenly a lot of folks came in and started claiming it was theirs.*"

"*I have my passport with a visa to classical Greece right here, so let's just start looking, OK?*"

"*Why don't you go through this box. We have a lot of gloves—maybe what you lost is a glove? This has a name tag from one of the editors of the early editions of the* Norton Anthology of English Literature. *And here's*"—

"*No way. Today's genres are outside the box. Never mind—let me just leave and thank you for not finding what was lost.*"

Art Nouveau 1905

pleasure that mocks the measured—
    dream-
             ing   winking   dashing
                    flirting
    and flashing its skirts at yesterday's
rules lined up like uniformed schoolgirls.

Art Nouveau wouldn't know from maybe:
tendrils figure skate
        anapests tap dance into their sunrise
flowers on steroids
        washed down with red Burgundy
            embrace the whole doorway

        (and who knows what they get up to after dark).

While melancholy symmetries
Of next door's neoclassicism,
Long committed to balancing
The books and the buds,
Avert their hooded eyes
From Nouveau's flirtatious look,
And tighten their grip
On yesterday,
And on their tight-lipped anticipation
Of tomorrow's determined
Restorations and reversions.

Art History 101

A professor of architectural history, a neoclassical garland on its night off the building's facade, and an Art Nouveau iris from an adjacent building all walk into a bar. The iris flashes a smile and asks its neoclassical neighbor, "What's a nice garland like you doing in a poem like this?" while resting his stamen on her shapely berries. The neoclassical carving, too restrained to insult the iris to its facade or to any other listener, gently but firmly moves the stamen away while murmuring under its breath the insulting label being hurled at Art Nouveau in many quarters: "noodle style."

OK, so this is the sort of joke that has to start with their going into a bar, but bar or no bar some grandmother is in the kitchen cooking pasta, and the iris is served a plate of noodles. While he is just beginning to twist one gracefully around his fork, the architectural historian arranges for some heavies he knows to cart Art Nouveau off for barometric surgery. . . .

That architecture professor proceeds to explain his motive to the woman on the adjoining bar stool, a tramp who was hopefully flashing her goodies at the three newcomers. Art Nouveau, he intones, thumbed its nose at generations of tradition, trampling the neoclassical forms that are so proudly rooted in French patrimony, but the style is now being rapidly rejected and buildings being gratefully and gracefully transformed back to their earlier neoclassical dignity. The shady lady says she likes dignified older men and gives a special discount to professors. But a customer down from the celestial realms for a night on the town overhears those lies about architectural history: he knows that Art Nouveau is still alive and well on many buildings. This visitor was reading about Pinocchio to his kid just the other night, so in revenge for the lie he makes the nose of the art historian grow long roots and turn bulbous.

And then bulbous blooms into iris.

Sweet Dreams

Near naps unmap, these shores unmoor: transformed into quondam amphibian, I slip and slide and wade in this wildest of territories, this beach between sleep and waking. Sometimes thoughtoids graze on unfurling fronds, laid back, lazy. Words scamper solitary on the dunes of the mind, playing alone before they get serious and become the dialogues of dreams. *Surely there aren't eleven six-toed kittens and an adolescent dragon in our bedroom, I must be falling asleep*, I'm sentient and sensible enough to murmur to myself. Before beginning to feed the creatures my fingertips. For nightmares are kenneled on these borderlands too: their fragments uncage, not curled but coiled, goblins in training to be demons. My plotting sandman gets by the liveried doormen of the sandcastle by pretending to deliver nutritious Chinese food rather than spoiled and spoiling dreams, but I discover too late that all his white cartons, left at my door, were addressed to Pandora.

To Catch a Thief

Heather Paige Dubrow
(née Kent; born January 5, 1969) is an American actress and television
personality. She portrayed Lydia DeLucca in the television series
That's Life *in 2000, and starred on the reality television series*
The Real Housewives of Orange County *from 2012 to 2016.*
–Wikipedia

Doppelgangers circle job ads from "William Wilson." But "Heather"?
Surely they won't apply. And as for "Dubrow" plus "Heather"...

She swiped "Dubrow" from her husband, my identity from me.
"Nine-tenths of the law"? Mine since birth, Heather.

The Imposter is—gulp—on reality TV. She is
A Real Housewife of Orange Country. But damn it, I'm the real Heather.

An actress? So we've made our (same) name in such disparate ways:
Very different fields grow each of these two Heathers.

Imagine my students' glee when they Google me—poet,
scholar, teacher—and read that "Heather

Spills on motherhood and selling her house." "Lives in a
monster spread." "Appears on The Love Connection." Heter-

Onyms are "words with the same letters but different meanings."
We both wrote that book. But I write monographs and poetry. No doubt that Heather

Only tweets. Wait—am I just jealous because top chefs feed her,
Fan clubs cool her, and tropical suns heat her?

Forget fairness: I'm sure she thinks ghazal is what you do with fast food.
Plus she criticized Obama. Reasons enough to hate her.

This poem and this world have too many HD's. We don't need more.
So let's not end the way ghazals have ended hitherto.

Aubade For Our Early Evening

> Must business thee from hence remove?
> —Donne, "Break of Day"

I muse that such love at our age
is as improbable as a flowering cactus
when my arthritic knees and leaping thoughts stir
  before you may wake at dawn.

Our annual physicals yield subprime mortgages,
Time's winged chariot enters the Indy 500.
But I'll attend to our sleepy smiles,
  not the brakes giving way at dawn.

The territory between your shoulder blades
curves to cradle and protect the chin
I'll soon need to stick out at work.
  Surely it's still grey, not dawn.

The Times also crashes by our door, but let's hear it for
these instruments that link us here (though less frequently),
not those new instruments devised by young bankers
  who leave for work each day at dawn.

 We too must leave for the "real world"? But truth awakes
in our private bedroom, not in private bankers' lairs.
Yet brokers afford pet phoenixes and feast on packaged larks:
  disjunctive conjunctions making hay
    while the sun rises at dawn.

Nuclear Test Site (II), or, Damaged DNA

i. Minnesota Spring

Forsythia bush:
ticker-tape parade thrown by
spring for small town parks.

ii. Nevada Spring

Nauseated robins skulk
among silenced buds
as dawn and fallout drift down.

The Syntax of Insects

*Most spider mites have a habit of covering leaves, shoots, and flowers with
very fine silken webbing, produced from a pair of glands near the mouth.
The silk strands aid in dispersal by allowing the mites to spin down from
infested to noninfested leaves, and to be blown by wind currents.*
–University of Kentucky College of Agriculture
http://www.ca.uky.edu/entomology/entfacts/ef438.asp

What masters of metaphor these spider mites are: they too make
connections, bridges, transported with the determination to
transport. Arachne and Charlotte had nothing on *Tetranychus urticae*
when it comes to infrastructures. And they would give Gandhi and
Mother Theresa a run for their selfless poverty in any competition
to help others. They nest downy pillows in crevices to permit their
troops a little R&R between forays. And then they engineer their
bridges from leaf to leaf so that other members of the battalion can
readily travel for their assaults.

Our garden plants and our re-pottings are colonized by these
plottings. From their perspective, how assuasive the crevices, how
auspicious the bridges, and then how delicious the leaves. Satan
wished global warming on that first garden, and straws may send
the camel howling to its orthopedist. But who would have thought
filaments as soft as rose petals, as fine as gold filigree could snake
around and kill my fragrant rosemary?

Cemetery of Lost Plots

The bookshelf of all these unsettling plots that could have been written instead is on its tiptoes, preening, careening. It's ready willing and able to tip over on anyone foolish enough to try to pull out a novel alternative to the set, the settled. There went the bride all dressed in white, but if only she had walked down a different aisle and shopped more shrewdly rather than being shopped—no, don't open the cans of worms on sale at half price on these gleaming shelves. (And in all fairness remember that her father hadn't read the subsequent chapters when he gave her away.) The shelf life of lost chances is long, the swelling of such cans should alert us to the toxins nurtured in their fertile though tinny wombs. But such warnings are seldom heard by those with tin ears, seldom read even by those who knock down one bookshelf after another as they try to grab a future whose flirting droplets pretend to give birth to rainbows.

The city pigeon

flaunts its neon green necklace—
as flashy as the hawkers whose corner it haunts.
Its grey? the shade of slush, not of dusk,
and strident stripings of rust intrude
on whites that should be sent to the laundry.
It sounds like a fire truck with a bad cold.
As for its shambling, you would be crazy
to trust it with the car keys without smelling its breath.

Admire these pigeons? Give me a break.
But pause just a second. Cool it when it coos.
Is this the music of rundown cities,
cracked violins played by those puddles and car fumes?
Or might our orchestras of pigeons proffer
song assuring and unassuming as comfort food?

Acknowledgments

I am grateful to the editors of the journals where versions of the following poems originally appeared: *AMP*: "Secrets Garden"; *Battery Journal*: "Application for Funding," "Art History 101," "Art Nouveau," "Boarding Calls," "Feral Dachshund," "Ghost in the Stroller"; *Chaffin Journal*: "Taking It With You"; *Deronda Review*: "Bedtime Stories, or, Commercial and Domestic Fragments," "Nuclear Test Site (II). Damaged DNA"; "Sweet Dreams"; *Ghazal Page*: ""Corporate Rodents," "Left Out to Dry," "To Catch a Thief"; *Inside Higher Education*: "Orange Harvest Moon"; *JuxtaProse*: "The Syntax of Bugs"; *Packingtown Review*: "Aubade for our Early Evening"; *Poem*: "Class Reunion," "Family Histories"; *Poetry Porch / Sonnets Scroll*: "The city pigeon"; *Poetry Salzburg Review*: "Mourning, Four Months Afterwards"; *Upstart*: "Lear's Fool," "Puck I. Puck to the Changeling Boy," "Strawberry Fields Forever"; *Yale Review*: "Here Comes the Bride."

I am very grateful to the entire staff of Cornerstone Press. Special thanks to these senior members of that team: Director and Publisher Ross Tangedal; Executive Editor Jeff Snowbarger; and two senior editorial assistants, Lindsey Bundgaard and Monica Swinick. The book was improved in many ways by the editorial insights and hard work of Tara Sparbel and Lindsey Strike; maybe you can't judge a book by its cover, but you can judge the design team, Ali Zamzow and Aleesha Splinter, by their splendid work on this cover. Both those groups were impressively led by Editor-in-Chief Johanna Honoré and

Managing Editor Colin Aspinall. It is also a pleasure to express my gratitude to my student assistant, John Miele.

Regrettably, I gave up writing poetry for nearly twenty years, influenced by a prejudice, widespread at the time though now at least alleviated, that one could not be a serious scholar of literature and a creative writer as well. So impressively led by Robert and Jana Kiely, Harvard's Adams House fostered a deep commitment to the arts and in so doing issued me a visa to the lost world of being a poet. For my return to wearing the two hats of poet and literary critic, I am above all deeply indebted to my close friend and fellow poet John Hildebidle and to the creative writing faculty at the University of Wisconsin-Madison. Members of that group warmly welcomed me into their circle when I was just beginning to write again, and I am especially grateful to Jesse Lee Kercheval and Ron Wallace.

For my work as a poet and so much else, I thank my domestic partner, Donald Rowe, to whom this book is dedicated.

Heather Dubrow, John D. Boyd, SJ, Chair in Poetic Imagination at Fordham University, is the author of *Forms and Hollows* and two chapbooks. Among the journals where her poetry has appeared are *Prairie Schooner*, *Southern Review*, *Virginia Quarterly Review*, and *The Yale Review*.

As literary critic, she has published seven single-authored volumes of literary criticism, a co-edited collection of essays, and an edition of Shakespeare's *As You Like It*.

She was director of Fordham's Poets Out Loud reading series from Fall 2009 to Summer 2020.